THE BURDEN WITHIN

Robert Burden's Journey from Prison to the Cross

An Uncensored Version

Compiled by
Birtie Finch
Copy Editor: Teresa Goins

authorHOUSE®

AuthorHouse™
1663 Liberty Drive
Bloomington, IN 47403
www.authorhouse.com
Phone: 833-262-8899

Published by AuthorHouse   04/25/2024

ISBN: 979-8-8230-2448-8 (sc)
ISBN: 979-8-8230-2447-1 (e)

Library of Congress Control Number: 2024906327

Print information available on the last page.

Contents

Introduction

by Birtie Finch

This book is about a man that I came to know from the small town of Owensboro, Kentucky. His given name was Robert Burden – for short, some call him Bob – but he now goes by the name *090902* in a Kentucky state prison. Bob was born in 1963 to Bobby Burden, Sr. and mother, Dorothy, and he has one sibling, Enus, his younger brother.

Bob's life story intrigued me because he continues to be able to get through another day knowing that, for all practical intents and purposes, his life is at the point of being over. I have always heard that God puts no more trouble on a person than he or she can handle, but in Bob's case, you will learn about the *burden within* – not only the burdens of the past that he has to carry every day but those that come from behind prison walls.

This account contains a lot of (let's call them) life situations that most of the readers of this book could never imagine. But one fact that many of us can agree upon is that no matter where we are in life – or how long, as in Robert's situation, that one might be separated from his family and friends (if there are indeed any family and friends left) – we end up looking for a way out. Some people turn to drugs and others, to sexual immorality, but many find themselves searching for a higher power. After 42 years of bearing his burdens, Bob chose to give them over to God, the only One who can truly free him from the pain and suffering he has endured since adolescence.

This narrative includes some graphic detail as well as some explicit language, as it was taken from an actual personal interview. As you go on this journey with Bob, keep in mind that the level of his education is not very high. Also, his intention is not to make you feel sorry for him or to elicit a handout. He only hopes that someone can benefit from the telling of his story and avoid the path he has taken. As you read through these pages, I ask that you not be too quick to judge but be openminded and grateful that (like Bob) we can take any problem, any situation – any *burden* – to a Heavenly Father, who is willing to fight our battles for us.

CHAPTER ONE

Looking Back

Thinking back to one of the happiest parts of my life growing up was riding in the back of an old F-150. I can still feel that air on my face, going down that ol' dirt road or new highway. My dad and the grownups would be up in the cab of the truck, and that was the best ride ever! I sure miss that. I know we can't replay our lives, but if so, I would make that part a "do over," as we called it. Also, hanging your legs off the tailgate was a bad thing to do because you could – and we *did* – fall off and get hurt. Luckily, we were never going too fast! So, all in all, I miss the smallest stuff. I sure have enjoyed so much life in my 60 years. It's been a hell-of-a-ride because I am still a kid at heart. I can let my mind go back and enjoy the ride.

Also, looking back as a kid growing up with my dad, one year, we were out digging for ginseng, which at the root, now goes for $800 a pound. (Back then, it was only worth $100 a pound, but at that time, that was a lot of money.) So, imagine this: We were digging the biggest patch ever, so, we got started, and I looked up, and my dad was gesturing with his hands. It looked like he was going crazy, smacking his face and such. Well, come to find out, there was a hornet's nest in that patch of ginseng! They came out stinging him and me, and my dad ran off, down the hill. I was running behind him, and I finally caught up to him, crying because it hurt so bad. The hornets had stung me all over my face, so, Dad took some tobacco and wet it, then put it on all the places where those bees had stung me. You probably won't believe this, but the wet tobacco stopped the hurting immediately! We didn't collect the ginseng right then but went back that winter and got that big patch of ginseng. And we had the biggest Christmas I had ever seen!

I often think back to my tenth birthday – even at 60 years old, I still do. It was February 14th, my big day. My stepmom Dot was telling my dad, Bobby, Sr., "Don't you dare forget this boy's big day! Bring his birthday cake home with you, or don't come home at all."

Dot was not the one you played with, believe me. All day, I looked up that ol' dirt road, waiting for the old man to bring me a store-bought cake. No disrespect toward Dot, but it wasn't going to be her usual homemade cake (although it was tastier).

Then, as night fell, I got sleepy, so, Dot made my pallet on the floor, as she always did, for the simple fact that we were short on beds. I liked my bed because of all of Granny's homemade blankets. But my dad had let me down once again, so, I cried a bit until I finally fell asleep.

Then, in the middle of the night, I woke up to a commotion. Dot was mad as hell! I heard her screaming, "Get out, get out!"

In my heart, the old man had it coming. I was even a bit happy because he was finally in deep shit, so, back to sleep I went. It was about 2 or 3 a.m. that he had come back home – drunk as Cooter Brown – falling-down drunk!

Anyhow, Dot told me he tried to start a chainsaw next to my homemade bed, and guess what I did? I jumped up and almost ran through a plate-glass door, but my Aunt Betsy stopped me. Dot immediately started giving the old man hell, and he and one of his drinking buddies went outside, then, came back in with a big box *full* of all kinds of cakes you could think of! There were over a hundred cakes, last count!

Then, my dad said to me, "Damn it, boy! Here is your birthday cakes forever and ever, at least for the next 100 years, so, don't never let me hear you not getting a cake the rest of your sorry life!"

But being a kid, I was so happy that the ol' S.O.B. had been out at a bakery, rolling dice that were loaded, and he had won all of them cakes. They said he cleaned the bakery out! You can't make this up – ol' S.O.B. has me *still* getting my cakes paid up! Damn, ol' dice game!

I do still think of my time as a kid growing up, but the moments I shared with my dad were always short-lived. He drank and drugged a lot; sometimes, it seemed like always, but when he wasn't substance abusing, he was the best dad a kid could ever have. He took me fishing, as well as hunting. He also schooled me about the outdoors, mainly the woods, to the point where it became my second home. I believe to this day that I could make it a long period of time in the outdoors. Work was also important, but to my dad, school was the most important thing a guy could do.

My dad only told me he loved me a few times; it was just "words" the rest of the time. I had to look for that love in his face – funny thing, huh? But now, as a man, I don't do that with others I love – just don't know why that is. When Dad was drinking and drugging, he beat me like a grown man. He would hit me and just like that, I would be in the hospital. Most of the time, he would say that I looked so much like that "bitch of a mother" I had. That hurt because she gave me up at one year old, when Child Protective Services came to get me. They got me out of a pail in my dad's home. He was drunk, as usual. When I got older, my grandma (my dad's mom) told me that my diaper was so stuck to my skin that it had to be cut off at the hospital.

For years, I hated him for that. He beat me till that day I killed him! My heart remains broken. I still love you, Dad!

CHAPTER TWO

Special Moments

Back in 1979, I enjoyed a certain special moment in my life. I was living with my grandmother at the time, and three doors down was a girl named Cathy, who had a brother by the name of Frankie, who was paralyzed from the waist down. So, as usual, I was drunk and high – a trait I inherited from my dad – and it was Halloween night, and I found my way to Cathy's house. I remember Frankie laying there in bed smiling, as he always did. While looking at him, my drunk ass came up with this great idea to take Frankie trick-or-treating.

I remember Cathy telling me, "No, you can't," that he had never been trick-or-treating before. But Frankie was just looking up at me, smiling from ear to ear – like it was Christmas – saying he wanted to go.

So, what did I do? Against Cathy's will, I got Frankie in that wheelchair – it took an hour or so, seeing that the boy weighed 350 pounds! It was cold out that night, and he wanted his jacket. He was ready to go, you could tell! So, I took him to every house within a four- or five-block radius. We didn't miss a door!

People asked what he was dressed up to be, and I would smile and answer, "Well, he's playing paralyzed and handicapped from the neck down."

Then, people would dump the whole bucket of candy in Frankie's lap, and he loved it! What sticks in my head most is getting him home and back in bed with a garbage bag plum-full of candy, watching him smile from ear to ear, his sister wiping chocolate from his face. Frankie looked at me with a smile that I had never seen before. Right then and there, I knew he and I had had the time of our lives that night!

Until this day, I know that had to be one of the best days of Frankie's life. Sad to say, he passed away two years later. As I staggered my drunk butt home that night, I felt tears of joy running down my face. I know that he is looking down on me now from heaven, smiling as this is being written down … and hopefully, he is eating a sticky chocolate bar!

I had one more special moment that occurred right before the episode with Frankie. It was in the mid-70s when I was about 16 years old … and so was she. Her name was Suzie, and we met in a subdivision. I, of course, was from "the other side of the tracks," and it was summer-time when we met. She was five-foot-eight with brown hair and blue eyes. She probably weighed about 135 pounds. She was dark-complected and smelled like teen spirit. We got to talking, and she gave me her phone number. This was on a Thursday. Later, I called her, and she told me her parents would be gone from Friday until

Sunday, so, she said that I could come over and stay with her in their nice subdivision. I told her that I would be there.

Well, I got there Friday night around 8 p.m. She opened a sliding door, and there I was, standing in a white jumpsuit, smiling. She was real tan and pretty, and I got a hug and a kiss on the cheek and walked on in. I had about a gram of blonde hash and a fifth of *Cold Duck* champagne. At 16 years old, I thought I was doing something!

So, we sat and smoked a couple of pipes-full while we listened to Bob Seger's *Night Moves*. You will never believe this part, but she invited me to her bedroom! We opened the door, and the night light was on, shining a pink beam of light over the entire area.

The whole room was decorated in pink, including the canopy bed! I kind-of laughed, and she said, "Don't say nothing because you're still going to get lucky." I just couldn't believe that at 16, she was still sleeping on a pink canopy bed!

We got undressed with Bob Seger playing in the background. She told me that this was her first time, and I thought to myself, "*Sure*," but little did she know, it was also my first time. I didn't let her know that, though. I made her think I was experienced and told her it was alright – I would "drive the car." I was just as scared as she was. I was a little clumsy when I started the process until I felt her skin break. Then, I realized what was going on.

After we had sex, we rolled over, and the bed felt extra wet, so, we turned the lights on, and there was blood everywhere. Suzie freaked out and asked what was she going to do because her mom was going to be upset. I asked her if she had a washer and dryer, and she did, so, I washed and dried the sheets, and all the stains came out. She quit panicking, and we went to the living room and started laughing and cuddling, and I felt relieved. We smoked some more hash and were drinking the *Cold Duck* when the sliding door opened, and a big guy came in (who happened to be Suzie's brother).

Hurriedly, he said, "Suzie, what are you doing? Mom and Dad are on the way home right now!" So, we had to clean everything up … and that was the end of that night.

Sadly, Suzie and I never had sex again, but we stayed in contact on the phone. Then, her family moved to Texas, but a year later, they came back to Kentucky. I was working at *Dunkin' Donuts* with my new girlfriend, and she said that Suzie was on the phone and wanted to say hi.

I said, "Of course," and got on the phone.

We started talking, and Suzie said, "You were my first, and I will never forget that, if I live to be 100 years old."

We kind-of laughed, and my girlfriend sort-of punched me in the arm, so, I told Suzie I had to go but to give me a call.

Damn, that ol' pink canopy bed and Bob Seger – what were you trying to do to me! *Night Moves*, really? Note to self: Quit looking at sales ads for furniture because every time you see a canopy bed, you think of her!

CHAPTER THREE

The Monster

At 16 years old, I spent most of my time working a parttime job or fishing and doing other outdoor stuff. One day, my step-uncle was over at the house. He was so messed-up in the head that he was always trying to put his hands on me and the other kids (and not in a good way but a sick way). So, I had asked him a few times not to put his hands on me, but then, one day, he tried to grab my butt and my "little dude" ... and that's when I knew I was becoming the Monster that I hated so much.

I got out a .38 pistol, and I shot my uncle two times – once in his face and the other, in his chest. I went to kid prison at the age of 16 years old, until I was 18 ... and now, we will get to the rest of the story. (I thought at 16 years old, I was supposed to have, or should have been having, *fun*! But that was not at all fact! S.O.B.!)

As you may have already suspected by now, in 1982, I killed my dad – God rest his soul. He beat me all my life. He hit me in my face like you would a grown man. This went on from about the time I was five years old, until I killed him. So, to *kill* the Monster, I *became* the Monster! My dad's drinking was a big part of his hurting me (and in the process, hurting himself). I forgive him now for what he did to me all those years, but I will never forget it.

The day I killed him was just like most of my days. I was drinking and doing whatever drugs I could do in one day. That's when the Monster surfaced – and that was the day that I took my dad's life. Before I realized what I was doing, I had pulled his body up into a "walk-in" drain – that's just how *big* the drain was. And after I killed him, I sat with his body for over a week. The smell was so bad that I will never forget it! I can still see the maggots coming out of his face! God, forgive me! Like I said, to kill my Monster, I became a Monster, at the age of 18 years old. *Damn!*

Fast-forward a few years, and in November of 1986, James Robert Burden *090902* was convicted of the kidnapping, rape, and murder of a woman. (There was an accomplice, but Bob stuck to the code that most criminals live by, which is no ratting or snitching.) Burden was sentenced to life in prison, plus 20 years, for kidnapping and murder, and 10 years for manslaughter – a total of life, plus 30 – while already serving a 17-year sentence for another kidnapping and robbery. By now, I (Burden) realize what needs to happen to the Monster. He must be stopped by all means, either caged up or put to death. And I know that it must end with me!

CHAPTER FOUR

Prison Stories

When I first got here [prison] in the early 1980s, the yard was pretty much segregated. Around 80 percent of the blacks and other races were located in the "bottoms." Even the chow hall lines were like that – one side was mostly blacks, and the other, mostly whites. It's not like that today. At one time, they painted yellow squares on the chow line floor, and if you weren't standing in one of those squares, you were considered to be bucking the line, which carried 15 days in the hole. I know I learned the hard way!

A friend of mine – whose name I will call by his initials, which are W.C. – made the best home brew (*Hooch*) in the prison system at that time. W.C. became a Christian and has been an avid Christian for 20 years now. I mean, he has been a Christian one-hundred percent (100%) and hasn't faltered at all! The reason I'm writing this is that you have to remember where you came from but not stay there in it. No, sir, I am not tough – or a bad ass – I am just old-school.

Around about 1987, Billy came in and got himself in a big debt (inside the prison walls) for dope. He couldn't pay the debt, of course, and the dudes he had gotten the dope from wanted a pound of flesh for what he owed. As a result, I heard Billy scream for over a year!

One day, he came to me and asked, "How do you turn prison off?"

I told him that basically, you leave what happens in prison and get out of there, get a good woman, and start a good life. He told me that if he ever came back [to prison], he would *kill* himself! I told him that killing himself would be a bad idea.

Well, Billy got out, and we stayed in touch for about a month; then, after about three months of not hearing from him, I finally got in touch with his sister. She told me that he had gotten arrested for a DUI and was put in jail, and he hung himself, just like he said he would. Now, when I walk past Dorm 8, I can still hear him scream! Ain't that crazy? I've done 42 years in prison and still hear that scream …

So, I met this guy in prison named Frankie (a different Frankie, not the 350-pound paralyzed Frankie from before). He was 17 years old but charged as an adult, and he had a speech impediment, so, over the next 18 years, I raised him as a son that I never had on the streets. And I noticed over time when Frankie would eat that he would put his arm around his food, like he was guarding it, and he would eat real fast and never get full. He would even ask me if I was going to finish my food, so that he could maybe finish it, and I would tell him to slow down, that nobody was going to take his food from him.

He would smile and say, "Okay, Bo" (he called me "Bo"), but would continue on, guarding his food with his life.

So, one day, I said to him, "You haven't been in prison that long. Why do you eat like that?"

Frankie explained to me that his parents died in a car wreck when he was young, and he went to live with his uncle (his dad's brother) and his wife, who had three kids of their own. So, what would happen is that when his uncle would leave for work, and his aunt would cook a meal, she would make Frankie sit and wait on the couch – watching her and the kids eat.

Then, when they were finished eating, his aunt would tell him, "Come on, dog. You get the scraps. Come eat."

So, Frankie looked at me and said, "Bo, I wasn't a dog. I don't know why she treated me like that."

I told him, "No, you're not a dog. You're a lot better than that." To my comment, Frankie kind-of smiled, but I could always see a tear in his eye when we would talk about it.

One day, his uncle came home and saw what was going on, and after that, Frankie bounced around from home to home and jail to jail. I explained to him that one day, he wouldn't have to worry about being treated like a dog anymore because he would eventually be "home" in the Land of Milk and Honey, in heaven.

He asked me, "How *much* milk and honey they got up there?"

I told him, "Plenty."

He said, "Oh, good, cause I sure would eat all I could."

I often think of Frankie. Mostly, when I start to pity myself, I just think about Frankie's life. Sometimes, the smallest things mean a lot to someone else. I know that when we all get up to where we are going,

I can only hope to see Frankie smile and eat all he wants! Thank you, Lord, for the *Frankies* in my life.

I was working in the diet kitchen at the old Kentucky State Reformatory (KSR), smoking a cigarette and cutting up grapefruit for the diet trays. And – *allegedly* – this is what happened …

While I was working, this inmate kept bothering me, and I kept telling him to leave me alone. Well, he didn't, so, I chased him around our area with a long knife. As I was about to stab him, he jumped the steam table – just another minute, and he would have been "grave-yard" dead! On top of that, there just so happened to be a black guy and a member of the NAACP on the yard. So, when my "hole" time was up – for what I had *allegedly* done to the NAACP dude and the Muslim community of the yard – they contested and complained about me getting out of the hole. The funny part about all of this was that at the time, I was a member of the NAACP, and I had many friends that were Muslim. One of my best friends is originally from Iraq. Imagine that!

There was a guy in Dorm 8 on C-Walk that had a five-year sentence. I don't know what for, but he had three months to go until he got out. He called home, but instead of his wife answering his call, *Jody* answered. "Jody" is the slang term for another male figure that has "moved in" while you are in prison. This guy went to his cell, broke the key off in his door, and hung himself with a cable cord. Hanging there, his skin turned all different colors. He only had three months before getting out. Such a shame …

I often get asked what a guy does as far as a relationship goes (both emotionally and physically) in prison. So, I could give you many examples of relationships, including straight and bisexual, but I'll give you an example of a good relationship I had.

So, I met this guy. He was in his twenties, and I was in my late fifties. His bi-name was Trish. So, basically, we would get high and eat together, and the sex was exceptional – neither of us had any complaints. I really don't condone same-sex relationships, but there's not much to choose from in a life behind these walls, so, I guess this was a time I was living in sin.

So, me and Trish were together for about a year. We got close on all levels, in a lot of ways. One of the biggest things in a friendship is keeping it real and being honest, but he couldn't because he had an addiction to drugs, and most people with addictions will lie, cheat, and steal, just to feed that addiction. But when an addiction gets to the point of jeopardizing one's health and safety, you have to let that person go (but you can still keep him in your heart).

The last six months of our relationship, we fought verbally and physically – I mean, it came to where I was blacking his eyes once a week because he would disrespect me (and himself). So, the final straw – I mean, the breaking point – came one day when we were sitting on the yard drinking home brew. He lived in Dorm 3, and I lived in Dorm

1. We got into a fight in front of about five others that were "Lifers" like me. He took off, and the other guys looked at me and told me to handle it, or else, they would handle it. So, I did. But first, let's go back a few months earlier …

So, basically, we had been ignoring staff direction – everyone knew about Trish and me – and you just don't get involved in prison relationships! It got so bad that at a point, he (Trish) was so strung out that I would have to help him clean up after he would use the bathroom on himself. It was heart-breaking. So, after he got halfway clean of the drugs, he would tell me about his life on the streets and about his family, and I liked listening to his stories. His family always thought that he would make a good preacher.

So, anyways, we were in a two-man cell. He (Trish) would come sleep in my cell during the day while I was out at my State job because he felt safe there. So, one day, I came in and watched him sleep, all curled up. I would just wonder how this kid could throw his life away. So, now, let's go back to where we were …

I knew I had to handle this situation, or I would be disrespected if I didn't. So, I go and get my knife and follow Trish to his dorm, and I cut him just enough to please all my prison peers … which finally got his attention!

At the same time, it was going through my mind that I was actually scarring this guy's face up over some stupid prison respect issues! Till this day, I struggle with what I did. I still look at his picture from time to time. I guess he had to have plastic surgery.

I often think, "*Did I have to do that?*"

Then I answer myself, *"Yes, I did, because if I hadn't, I would have been on the receiving end!"*

So, nowadays, I ask myself, *"Am I still the Monster I became the day I killed the Monster?"*

As I was leaving Trish's dorm that day, I took a lock to the head and a knife to the gut. The officers also busted me because I had a knife, and I went to segregation. I didn't rat, and neither did Trish, so, basically, what we did was take our issue to church.

A week or two afterwards, a man on the yard asked me if I wanted to let him go home. He asked me, "Can I go home?"

I told him, "Yea, go home," and after that, I saw him start actually going to church! I guess he found Jesus.

What I like to stay is that I have been stabbed and cut and also, have done the same, and I'm not proud of it, nor am I ashamed. But this hurt. The look on this man's face who wanted to "go home" will never leave my mind (again, I can't make this shit up).

One day when the State was in charge of the kitchen, an officer named Bruce was breaking up a fight that had happened in the bakery. One of the guys involved was a friend of mine, and he stood about six-foot tall. He only had a five-year bit to do, so, Bruce stepped in and grabbed the smallest inmate, who was about five-foot-seven-inches and pinned him against the bakery wall. My friend picked up a dough hook (which weighed about 50 pounds) and was in the process of swinging it, with the intentions of hitting the smaller guy. As Bruce turned around to block the swing, I stepped in, and my arm caught the brunt of the dough hook.

The question here is, "What were my intentions, and who was I trying to save that day?"

For one, my friend would have gone to death row. Two, Bruce would not have gone home to his family. Third (and last), the smaller guy had a look of relief on his face. To sum up this story, 15 days for fighting is a lot better than death row!

Bruce said, "I'm going to get some good time for you," and, "I'm going to write a letter for you," but it never materialized.

As I told him, "I don't need either one." Being human was enough.

CHAPTER FIVE

Unconditional Love

Let me tell you about my granny. Her love for me was so unconditional, even after I was convicted of the killing of my father, who was her firstborn son! She told me that she forgave me. She said that she knew it had to have been an accident.

So, the short part of this story is that I was in the Eddyville, Kentucky state prison, in the hole, because I had escaped from another prison ... well, that's another story for another time. The captain came to my cell bars and told me that my grandmother was in ICU and asked me if I wanted to go to her funeral or to a bedside visit.

Well, they transferred me to Owensboro, Kentucky, so I could see my granny before she died. Two officers took me, even though I was a convicted murderer and an escape risk. They put me in a jumpsuit and shackled me with a black box. From the black box, a chain came through for my hands and feet, and now, I was ready, so, they put me in the cruiser, and off we went.

Three hours later when we got to the hospital, three Owensboro police with shotguns escorted me into the hospital. I mean, they cleared the whole floor of the ICU unit! It was just me, my granny, and the officers (and shotguns).

As I was standing in the room with my grandma, all I could do was stare at her. She had tubes that were running from her brain, pumping blood from a blood clot that had formed there. She was heavily sedated, in a coma-like state.

So, I'm standing there next to her bed, almost in tears, next to the women that showed me unconditional love, and I am thinking to myself, "*I took your son's life. How could you still love me and forgive me?*"

Like I wrote in another of my stories, "I *killed* a Monster and *became* a Monster."

After an hour of talking to my granny, pleading with her to wake up and talk to me, the police officers are now telling me that my visit is up – and to say my goodbyes.

So, at that point, I screamed as loud as a man could scream, "Mom, please, please, speak to me!"

Then, one last time, she opened her eyes and said, "What, lil' Bobby?" She closed her eyes with a small smile on her face, and the shotgun-wielding cops escorted me out of the hospital.

And the next thing you know – we couldn't have been more than two blocks from the hospital – over the cops' radio, they said, "Let inmate Burden know that Ms. Burden has passed away."

What little heart that I had left in my chest fell to my feet – part of me died that day – and I have never experienced unconditional love since, that is, until I accepted the Lord as my best friend. Now, He's never turned His back on me since! Even though I was a cold-hearted person, I have to say that that fact has changed my life.

I have often let myself think of my grandma, and I picture Angels walking with us, and that says a whole lot about my granny. She was *my* Angel! She is really the only one who I can say loved me emphatically, no strings attached.

I can hear her say, "Lil' Bobby, try not to stay out long. But if you do, remember that the lights will be on in my kitchen."

I can recall it like it was yesterday, seeing those lights on at our home, always on. Man, we had so much fun in that ol' kitchen. She would home-school me there, and I never really cared to listen. But years later, I can hear her sweet voice telling me that ol' "school stuff" that I truly use today – things like how to cook, bake, and can food up – I mean, everything that you need to know in the kitchen, inside and out.

I would ask her, "Granny, why are you pushing this girly stuff on me?"

She would tell me, "You'll see."

And sure enough, I did. Granny knew that most men back then were crazy and couldn't keep a good wife, so, if you didn't know how to feed yourself, you were just shit-out-of-luck! She was the most loving person in my entire life, which is why I know that she is my Angel!

I know she is looking down on me, and I can betcha' she is telling Jesus, "That's my grandson. Look how good he's doing." Man, she is pulling for me still!

"Angel, you are … Mom, if you can hear me, see ya. I'll be home soon. Just keep the lights on! Bo."

I had a dream about a convict.

A crown of thorns was on His head.

He came glidin' down the highway,

Right over to me, and said …

"Hey, don't you know me?

Don't you remember my name or my crime?

Well, I was busted and convicted, cut down in my prime,

When I came to help everyone do their time."

I tried to be cool, but I was shaking.

I couldn't walk; I couldn't see.

I said, "But I'm not one of your faithful, Lord,

So, why would you come to me?

"I mean, maybe, I'm not doing great,

But I figure, at least, I was doing fine.

And I'm a free man, do-as-I-please man,

So, what's all this talk about doing my time?"

And He said, "You can climb the highest mountain,

Swim the deep blue sea,

Roll around naked in money, Boy,

But you'll never be free.

"So, I've come to assist you,

If you're willing to learn how to let your light shine.

But I've had so many faces and names

(Don't get hung up in religious games).
You just gotta learn how to love everybody,
All of the time."

I said, "But Lord, my brother's in prison,
And you know my back hurts all the time.
And my daddy died; baby sister can't stop drinking that wine;
Politicians cheat and steal; look what you're asking me to feel.
I'm sorry. I respectfully decline."

Then, without another word, He touched my heart,
And I felt something crack apart,
Like a door that hadn't opened in some time.
I saw the earth and everyone on it;
I saw His Light all over me,
The good in everybody, I saw it the way He must see.

And I felt His love for it all
And how He marks every sparrow's fall,
And how sorrow always has its reason and rhyme.
He let His hand fall to His side,
And I cried and cried and cried.

And He said, "Now, let's take it from the top
About doing your time.
If you've got a cross, then I can bear it,
But you gotta seek if you wanna find.

"Get a song, then try to share it,
But try to be simple and try to be kind.
And don't get carried away by the things that pass every day;
Just try to keep my peace in your heart and mind."

That's all my Gospel, and it's true
Because all you really need to do
Is be loving to everybody, all of the time —
My Born-Again Blues …

CHAPTER SIX

Keeping It Real

As I recall, years ago, prison life was a lot different. When someone gave you his word, that was more than money could ever get you. All you could be was who you were, as long as you stood on your feet and your word. But nowadays, that's not true. Most of these guys just can't keep it real or just be who they really are, always putting on an act for the next man or just being flat-out liars to me. Only if they knew that it is so much easier keeping it real and being truthful with each other.

The things to me that last are just lost in the past. I don't ask why or try to figure it out anymore. I believe that most guys think that life owes them something, for whatever reasons. I remember when I used to feel and think like that, but as I manned up, I had to set aside my childish ways and realize that I owed myself a better life, full of happiness. It is so sad at times to see this attitude in people, but at least I can see it. It's almost like reading a book.

Over the years, I ask the new guys (often called "Fish"), "Why do you keep coming back to prison?"

Some of the best answers I get are, "I eat well here, better than I do in the streets," and, "There are absolutely no bills, just free everything!"

I look … I just look at them and then, I ask myself, "*What the hell are these kids thinking?*"

I can never see prison as a good thing. I would enjoy freedom too much, and I don't even have an "out" date. But there is one thing I can say: I truly have freedom in my heart. (But I still think about how wonderful it would be to just be able to walk through the park or eat whatever food I see fit to eat – no State prison food at all.) I look at a lot of these newcomers, and most of them are just lazy or settling for a free ride. But what the hell ever – not me!

I can't make this up, man. "Grow up! Freedom is not only outside these walls but it's definitely in your heart, so, my advice to you young guys – if you don't want to be labeled a "Fish" – get a job … a J.O.B.!"

I often hear men on the phone say out loud, "Fuck you!" or "Go to hell!" They even call whomever is on the phone "Bitch," or they say, "Get my money in," or a whole lot of other dumb stuff.

Then – and this takes the cake – at the end of the phone call, they're saying, "I love you, Mom [or whomever they're talking to]."

Man, I can't believe *anyone* would take a call or help someone after *that!* These Fish don't realize that no one owes us anything.

"Grow up and be grateful, Fool!" Imagine that …

In 2004 (or maybe later on), I met a brother named Carl. He was about six-foot-two and 200 pounds. Big ol' boy! He was doing Life for murder. At the time, we were working for Prison Industries (P.I.) at the KSR prison.

While on break, just sitting and talking about everything under (and over) the sun, Carl looks over at me and tells me, "Bo, don't ever let anyone rob you of your happiness, and most of all, your joy. You are good people. Stay real! Keep on being 'Bo.'"

Anyway, a man came up and said, "Carl, you got to go help unload the truck, A.S.A.P."

So, Carl got up, but as he was walking away, he turned, looked at me, and said, "Bo, remember what I told you."

Well, about 10 or 15 minutes later, all hell broke loose! Everyone was running back to the loading dock. Carl was down. They told us his heart just stopped … and the last person he talked to was ol' Bo.

Man, I can still see him walking, singing to himself. That's some real messed-up shit!

Between the killing and raping, of the crime itself, I've now been in prison [by this time] over 35 years, and I've seen it all, I guess, but also, a little good in life, not just in prison but the free world.

Sometimes, I have to tell myself, *"Brother, your whole life, they have called you 'white trash' or 'dope head,' and you listened!"*

Yes, I've done a lot of ugly stuff to others and hurt a lot of people – in here and outside. And I ask myself, *"Have I changed?"*

Well, truthfully, I don't know, other than this:

I don't need a drink or a joint to get through the day, and I don't hurt myself no more (or anyone else, if I can help it). I am the same guy, just too old for the B.S. Now, I just keep it real and simple.

Will this get me out of prison? *Hell, no!* and not anything else! But freedom is *inside* a man. I believe that riches can be defined as how you live each day for yourself and with others. Hell, I guess I am new at loving life and just keeping it real. *How about you?*

CHAPTER SEVEN

Angels Don't Always Have Wings

Well, I will start with my Higher Power that has always had an impact on my life, even as a kid. I think back to when I was 21 years old, facing the death penalty. I recall asking God to "take me." I want the readers of this book to listen to its writings as if I was sitting right beside you, telling you all of this in person ... because when the world says, "No," God says, "Yes."

My Higher Power was with me then and is with me now. When no one tried to see the good in me (or even care), He loved me 100 percent and still has my back, "paid in full." Listen to the words of God. Following are some of the passages that He brought to me in my times of need. And I will tell you the same thing Jesus told a woman who had committed adultery. "I don't condemn you! Go and sin no more!"

✝ "You are free to experience My unconditional love for you and leave your life of sin and pain" *(John 8:11. Romans 2:4; 5:18; 6:14-16; 8:1)*.

I know most likely that I will die behind these prison walls, but *I Am Free* in my heart! Now that I look at it, God has actually taken me from Death to Life! See, I know God has a reason. God sees our hearts, not our sins.

✠ "You are my child. You belong to me, for I not only created you; I also redeemed you when I died on the cross for all the sins of the world" *(John 1:1-4, 14; 3:16-17. Colossians 1:12-16. Galatians 3:10-13; 4:4-5. 1 John 2:2)*.

Now, God comes first in my life because I love Him first, before anyone or anything! He is my best friend. He's got my back. He loves me for who I am, but guess what? He's got *your* back, too! Just ask Him one time.

Just say this: "Father, you got my back for real! Just like you got Bo's."

And He will tell your heart, "Yes, I do." Just like Ol' G's, it don't cost a dime! He has paid for us *all* – not just a few – *all of us* – so, keep love in your heart.

✠ "But if you want Me to be your Saviour, you will not be disappointed. You will experience love that casts out fear, peace that passes understanding, and joy that no one can take away" *(1 John 4:17-19. Philippians 4:6-7. John 16:22)*.

✠ "When you are tempted to satisfy your cravings in unhealthy ways, I will enable you to have self-control and remind you that the blessings I give you will truly satisfy" *(1 John 2:15-16. Galatians 5:23. John 4:14. Philippians 4:4-19)*.

✠ "I will enable you to be patient with others as they are growing, and I will transform you so that kindness, compassion, and forgiveness flows from within" *(Galatians 5:22. John 7:37-39. Romans 12:2. Ephesians 4:32)*.

✝ (Now, I truly know that God has never lost a battle. He does all things but fail!) "When you are mistreated, misunderstood, or taken advantage of, your natural desire will be to seek revenge. Choose instead to allow Me to discipline those who have hurt you. While doing so, I will also seek to reach their hearts" *(Romans 12:17-21. Hebrews 12:5-11. Revelation 3:19. Luke 4:32).*

If you haven't figured it out by now, Mr. Burden has been wandering in his wilderness for over 42 years – just a little bit longer than the children of Israel. Deuteronomy 1:6 says, "You have dwelled on this mountain long enough." When God tells you to break camp and move out to face a challenge that He gives you, will you be ready to obey – ready to obey – or will you continue to wander in your wilderness? The way I see it, God never gives up on us. We give up on Him. And that's when the world says, "No," but God continues to say, "Yes."

So, Father, I want to thank you so much for sending me a wingless Angel in Miss Birtie. You always know when and where to place your angels around us humans.

Miss Birtie, may your cup runneth over with many blessings and joy and love. You have been a positive force in my life by taking a chance on me – not even knowing me but being willing to share my story. God bless you and your family. And then, when we all get to heaven, we will get to see each other's wings!

Kentucky Innocence Project dated October 31, 2023.

─────── COMMONWEALTH OF KENTUCKY ───────

KENTUCKY INNOCENCE PROJECT

DEPARTMENT OF PUBLIC ADVOCACY • 5 MILL CREEK PARK, FRANKFORT, KENTUCKY 40601
502-564-8006 • 502-695-6768 (fax) • Securus 165 • www.facebook.com/KentuckyInnocenceProject

CONFIDENTIAL – ATTORNEY/CLIENT PRIVILEGE

October 31, 2023

James Burden, #090902
Lee Adjustment Center
168 Lee Adjustment Center Drive
Beattyville, KY 41311

      RE: Attorney/Client Meeting

Dear Mr. Burden:

I am meeting with you in-person on November 2 at 12:30 p.m. We will discuss the Court of Appeals ruling, and upcoming parole hearing.

I have enclosed the Court of Appeals opinion in your case. They have agreed with us, and have granted your DNA testing. Your case will be remanded back to the Daviess Circuit Court to release the evidence and begin the testing process.

Before the case can continue into DNA testing a few appellate deadlines need to run to make the Court of Appeals opinion final. The Commonwealth has 20 days to ask for a rehearing of modification of the ruling, and 30 days to seek MDR to the KY Supreme Court after any rehearing or medication is ruled on by the Court of Appeals. Page six of the opinion is incorrect, and we will be seeking modification to remove page six from the opinion within those 20 days. I anticipate the Commonwealth will also seek rehearing and then MDR to the Supreme Court, but we will not know for sure until the deadlines have passed. I will keep you updated as those deadlines expire.

Once all motions are completed with the appellate courts, we will go back to the Daviess Circuit Court and get the testing process started. There is still much to work out on where we will send the items for testing, and that will determine how long the testing may take to complete. Once the items are sent to the lab, it can take anywhere from four to twelve months to complete the testing, depending on what lab is conducting the testing. We will be seeking testing from a private lab, Bode Technologies, in hopes of getting the best results possible.

Conclusion

by Birtie Finch

You may be asking yourselves what made me publish a writing about someone other than myself. Well, the reason is that God directed me to Mr. Burden's path. Yes, I could have written about all my trials and tribulations, but sometimes in life, you have to put others first (just like Ol' Bo said), and I quote:

"When God tells you to move off your mountain, will you be ready?" (Deuteronomy 1:6).

I believe that Mr. Burden's story can and will help someone whose heart needs to be free from sin or whatever stronghold has him or her bound. So, with that being said, I pray that someone will be there for *You* to help carry *Your* ***Burden Within*** …

God Bless You!

Keep on loving each other as brothers and sisters. Don't forget to show hospitality to strangers, for some who have done this have entertained angels without realizing it! Remember those in prison, as if you were there yourself. Remember also those being mistreated, as if you felt their pain in your own bodies.

Hebrews 13:1-3 (NLT)

Old Family Photos

Burden's dad (left), uncle (right)

Burden's dad and stepmom

Robert and Enus as children

Burden: Then & Now

Age 18   **Age 60**

James Robert Burden

090902

Burden's Hometown

Owensboro, Kentucky

Made By His Hands

Poem by Robert Burden

You are a work of art – made by His hands!

YOUR LIFE MATTERS!

And it all starts with

YOU!

Love yourself,

So that you can love others.

FORGIVE,

So that you can be forgiven.

TRUST

In yourself,

But most importantly,

In HIM!

Crosses
Made by Other Inmates

WOVEN CROSSES

← Knitted
with fibers
from sock fabric

Personalized →
and constructed from
strands of potato chip
bags and garbage bags

CROSS MADE OF SOAP

← Page from Bible
affixed to sculpture
(Book of Colossians)

The Popsicle-Stick Cross

Miss Birtie,

Good morning. It's 3 a.m., and I'm sending you this cross I carved from popsicle sticks. It took me about a week to cut it out.

This cross shows that even in here [prison], a person can be free in his heart. I am freer now, in here, than most people are on the streets. Jesus paid "in full" for all of us! I have tattoos all over my body of Jesus, my Saviour.

Anyway, Miss Birtie, I hope this will brighten your day and show you that, even in here, the Lord is working. If He can touch an old heart like mine, He can touch anyone's!

Know that you are loved in the Lord Jesus.

Bobby Burden

2023

This correspondence is representative of the handcrafted popsicle-stick cross depicted on cover of this book.

Acknowledgements

Book Compiled by
Birtie Finch

Birtie Finch is a member of Southern Star Missionary Baptist Church in Louisville, Kentucky. Her pastor and mentor is Reverend Dr. Barry C. Johnson, Sr., who baptized her in 2019. Birtie is devoted to her church and her membership in the Mass choir.

Birtie has served as a volunteer for the Louisville Elder Serve organization and the United Christian Hill Ministry. She has worked in a range of programs, including those that offer emergency finance, insurance, and food assistance to senior citizens. She has also worked for the Meals on Wheels community and organized various ecumenical activities for senior citizens groups.

Birtie's life turned around on March 15, 2010, when she gave her life over to the Lord.

Copy Editor:
Teresa Goins

"Thanks to everyone involved
for telling my story."

Robert Burden
2024

A video copy of an actual interview with Burden, recorded when he was 18 is available online. Please contact the Author if you want to purchase a copy.

Printed in the United States
by Baker & Taylor Publisher Services